976.4
KER

10.00

JUAN SEGUIN

A Hero of Texas

Rita Kerr

EAKIN PRESS
Austin, Texas

For my husband,
Larry Kerr,
and the children of Texas.

Contents

Preface		vii
Acknowledgment		viii
1	Home in Early Texas	1
2	The Battle for San Antonio	14
3	Messenger of The Alamo	26
4	Fighting at San Jacinto	40
5	Keeping The Faith	47
Bibliography		53

Preface

Texas had many heroes during the struggle for independence from Mexico. Names like Travis, Crockett, Bowie, and Houston are well known to all because they are prominently mentioned in history books. But there were other Texans who performed heroic deeds during the fight for freedom. They are rarely mentioned. One of these heroes was Juan Nepomucena Seguin. This is his story.

Acknowledgments

To Bernice Strong, Charline Pazliska, Sharon Crutchfield, Sandra Hall and Charles J. Long of the DRT Alamo Library, I owe a debt of gratitude. Without their help, it would have been impossible to obtain the historical information contained in this book. Thanks, too, to the librarians at the Texas Institute of Culture for their assistance.

Special thanks goes to B Sharp and Beverly Kemp for their suggestions and critique. Thanks go to family and friends who encouraged me. Finally, my sincere thanks to my husband for his advice and invaluable expertise in writing *Juan Seguin, A Hero of Texas*.

JUAN SEGUIN

A Hero of Texas

1

Home in Early Texas

Silently the band of men settled for the night in the old Spanish mission. They moved noiselessly and spoke in hushed whispers to avoid detection by the enemy that might be outside.

Juan Nepomucena Seguin leaned against the cold stone wall and closed his eyes. He relaxed in the peaceful stillness to let his mind wander back over his life.

He thought of his happy boyhood in their *hacienda* in San Antonio. But his fondest memories were of Casa Blanca, the rancho thirty miles south of town where they raised sheep and cattle. The homes of the *vaquero* families living there formed a large stockade for protection. In the center of the square stood the Seguin sandstone house. The San Antonio River was a short distance away.

During the early 1800s Indian raids were an ever-present danger. Like most children in Texas, Juan and his brother learned to saddle and ride a horse as well as

1

load a musket at an early age. Life was difficult in those days — even for people of wealth.

Juan recalled his twelfth birthday and the change it made in his life. Long before October 27th his father, Don Erasmos Seguin, had walked around smiling, with a twinkle in his dark brown eyes. Juan dared not question his papa. His father's word was law in their household.

Finally, the special day arrived. *"Felices cumpleanos,* happy birthday, Juan!" his family called as he entered the dining room.

His ten-year-old brother, Tomás, and his eight-year-old sister, Leonidas, sang the birthday song, *Las Mañanitas.* His mother's many petticoats rustled noisily as she stood on her tiptoe to kiss his cheek. "Happy birthday, Juanito," she whispered softly. Juan was tall and, like most twelve year olds, very shy.

Don Erasmos patted his son's shoulder while they found their places around the long, elaborately carved table. Maria, the family's cook, served hot chocolate and coffee. She had prepared Juan's favorite dish of fried bread dripping with wild honey.

"Pan dulce!" Juan exclaimed happily. After his second helping, he slumped contentedly in the leather-backed chair and licked his fingers.

Señor Seguin frowned. "You are almost a man, don't do that." He added. "You are too old for the usual birthday *piñata,* too."

Juan nodded. He would no longer be allowed to show his skill at breaking the paper-covered clay jar filled with sweets, but the knowledge that he was becoming a man eased his disappointment.

Don Erasmos took a brightly colored bandanna from the table and handed it to his youngest son. "Tomás, put this around your brother's eyes, then we will take him to his present."

2

His mother, Doña Josefa, smiled. "But be careful, do not get it too tight."

After tying the blindfold, Tomás checked to be certain it was attached securely. With giggles and laughter, the children guided Juan from the house, through the patio to the pasture behind the garden. Doña Josefa and her husband followed close behind. A small group of ranch workers and their children had come to watch the excitement. Birthdays were an important day on the rancho.

"Happy birthday, Son," Don Erasmos exclaimed while loosening the bandanna.

Juan trembled with anticipation, his heart beat wildly as he rubbed his eyes and looked around. His mouth flew open. There, in front of him, stood a handsome black pony with a fine silver-trimmed saddle. Raul, one of the ranch boys, had a broad grin on his tan face as he held the horse's reins. Juan stared from his parents to the animal. "Is she mine?" he whispered hoarsely.

"Son," his father laughed, "Every rancher needs a horse of his own! Yes, she's yours."

Juan stroked the pony's sleek head then walked around to inspect her from the tip of her soft wet nose to the end of her long black tail. He rubbed the hand-tooled saddle with his fingers and exclaimed, "Oh, *Papacito!* What a beautiful present. *Gracias!*" Tears of joy rimmed his brown eyes when he hugged his father. "*Mamacita*," he said looking down at his mother. "Isn't she the prettiest mare you ever saw?"

Señora Seguin, renowned for her exquisite beauty, beamed with pride. "*Si,* she is beautiful, Juanito." Her son bent to kiss his mother's cheek, he touched the jet black hair coiled around her head.

"She's a fine horse, all right," Tomás cried after completing his thorough inspection. "What will you name her?"

"You must call her Blackie," his sister insisted. "Look, she is all black but her white feet."

"That's too plain. Call her something pretty like Contessa." Tomás said, proud that he knew the word Contessa.

Juan shook his head. "I do not know what I will name her, I must think about it." His voice quivered. "May I ride her, Papá?"

Don Erasmos smiled, "*Si,* she is yours."

The boy slipped his boot into the stirrup of the saddle to swing onto the mare's back. He reached down for the reins and exclaimed, "*Gracias,* Raul."

All eyes were on the twelve year old. He shook the reins and bent to whisper softly into the horse's black ear, "Come on, girl. Let's show them."

Apparently the horse understood the importance of the moment. She lifted her white-stockinged feet daintily to prance around the pasture. Horse and rider blended into one as they paraded back and forth. A cheer of appreciation went up from the audience when the horse stopped in front of them. Juan felt he could explode with happiness as he slipped to the ground. His brown eyes were shining. He patted the pony's head. "Her name is *La Reina*. She is my queen!"

"La Reina, the queen," Leonidas cried. "I like that."

"Papá," Juan asked in a serious voice, "how old is she?"

Removing his *sombrero* to push a lock of black curly hair from his forehead, Don Erasmos answered. "Señor Flores said she would be three in the spring."

The excitement of the morning was over. One by one the spectators returned to their jobs and left the family alone. Doña Josefa sighed and reached for her daughter's hand. "Come, Leonidas and Tomás, it is time for your lessons."

4

Juan realized being twelve years old would have many advantages. He would no longer be required to attend classes when they were in town. Children ages six to twelve went to the school his father had founded in 1812. They studied reading, writing and arithmetic in Spanish, their native language. Señora Seguin taught her children when they were on the ranch and could not go to school.

In the weeks and months that followed, Juan and his horse galloped over the ranch. They were inseparable. With the passing months, boy and horse grew to maturity.

Early one morning in March of the year 1821, Juan walked from the house with an ear of corn for La Reina. He entered the stable and started into her stall. He stopped suddenly, then turned and raced back to the house. He waved his arms and shouted, "Papa! Papa! Come quick! Come quick!"

"I'm coming!" Don Erasmos called from the doorway. The boy's long legs raced back to the stable with his father right behind him.

Juan stopped at the entrance to the stall. "Look!" he cried softly. Nestled on the hay in the corner lay a newborn colt. La Reina nuzzled the baby proudly as it spread four gangly legs to stagger to its feet. Juan stood fascinated as the colt wobbled to its mother's side to nurse.

"Oh, papa, he knew what to do! Isn't he smart?" La Reina whinnied in agreement.

Señor Seguin nodded, he understood his son's pride.

"I will call him Prince!"

"That is a good name, son. A Prince for a queen, La Reina."

Prince grew quickly from the gangly all legs stage to

5

a frisky colt. The children spent many hours watching the pony.

One warm June evening, Don Erasmos and Juan were alone on the veranda. He cleared his throat and said, "Son, a group of Americans are coming to San Antonio to talk to Governor Martinez about bringing colonists to Texas. Baron de Bastrop has asked me to go with him to Nacogdoches to welcome the Americans and escort them back to San Antonio. I wish you would come with us."

Juan caught his breath. In the hush of darkness with the insects buzzing around them, Juan whispered loudly, "Really? I am going with you? What will Mama say?"

His father pushed the graying lock of hair from his forehead and explained. "She agrees. You are almost fifteen. You should take the trip but you will ride Chico. La Reina's still nursing her colt, she will stay here." There was a firm finality in his voice.

Juan's heart sank; how could he ride another horse? Yet, he realized such a long trip would be too much for Prince.

His father read his thoughts. "Tomás and Raul will look after your horses while we are away. Later, the family will take them to town. When we return we must have a big *fiesta* to welcome our visitors." He yawned and looked at the star-studded sky. "If we are to join Bastrop by mid-afternoon, we must leave early. So, let us go to bed." The two walked arm in arm into the house.

Juan was too excited to sleep. Before dawn the next morning he was in the pasture with his horses. Before he knew it, it was time to go.

Farewells to his family and the first day of journey were a dream to Juan. But, after sleeping wrapped in his *serape* on the hard ground the first night, he quickly settled into the routine. The party was on the way again before the first rays of sun could peek over the distant hills. The lead horses kept a steady gait while the pack donkeys, loaded with supplies, trotted along behind.

The second night on the trail, Bastrop remarked, "Tomorrow we will come to the Colorado River. We must find a shallow spot to cross; it is deep in some places."

The next day Juan understood his meaning. They had to ride a distance to find a place to ford the river.

Juan saw many things as they went along. He caught glimpses of buffalo grazing on the tall grasses. Once they surprised a deer and her fawn watering at a creek. The third day they saw Indian smoke signals on the mountains to the west. Mile after mile the country changed. The rolling hills flattened, then rose again. Mesquite and huisache trees were replaced by cypress and oaks along the riverbanks. In June the early spring rains were over, the shallow streams were easy to cross.

They watched for squirrels or rabbits for their suppers. Several times they stopped to fish in one of the creeks near where they camped. The men cooked the fish they caught by wrapping them in wet leaves and covering them with hot coals until they were cooked. Corn and tortillas with beans were basics at every meal.

At dusk the sixth day they rode into Nacogdoches and found the Americans in a *cantina*. Juan sat quietly listening to their talk. Baron de Bastrop, a Hollander by birth, a linguist by choice, served as translator. The spokesman of the visitors, Stephen Austin, had many questions about the land and people. Juan could tell he was eager to see Texas for himself.

After a day's rest to restock their provisions, the group set out. The return trip with the visitors was different. The Baron pointed out things Juan had never noticed; the richness of the dark soil, the thickness of the native grasses, and wild fruit trees and berries which grew along the trail.

Juan was fascinated with the English words. Two of the visitors noticed his interest and began exchanging their words for Juan's Spanish. The foreign language felt strange on his tongue, he had trouble with the *ch* sounds.

When they made camp, the men sat around the campfire to listen to the Baron talk about the land. "As you know Texas is part of Mexico. It is a big empty area. There are few people except in San Antonio and Nacogdoches. Elsewhere there are wandering Indian tribes that follow the herds of buffalo. Many of the people in Mexico live on ranchos and raise sheep; they have no desire to move north. The government wants more settlements in the woody places of Texas, especially along the rivers." He paused to catch his breath and continued. "Your father — my friend Moses Austin — was given a land grant to bring colonists to Texas to develop this wilderness. I was sorry to hear of his death."

"That is why I have come," Stephen Austin explained. "I promised my father on his deathbed that I would take his place. I want more grants to bring families from the United States to locate in areas assigned by your government. We will swear allegiance to your country and protect the land against hostile Indians." He yawned and stretched. "But if we are to start early in the morning we should get some sleep tonight."

Juan stared at the blanket of stars overhead and thought of all he had heard. He liked the thin, pale faced American, Stephen Austin, and his gentle, sincere manner.

The travelers kept a steady, even gait, and the days slipped by. When Juan realized they were nearing home, he became more eager with each passing mile. The afternoon of the sixth day he spied the twin towers of San Fernando Church near the *hacienda* and the arch on the old

8

deserted Spanish mission, the Alamo. The sound of their horses' hooves splashing through the San Antonio River covered the thumping of Juan's heart. He never dreamed he could be so eager to see his family.

Juan slowed Chico to stare at the thatched huts; everything looked so different. "Papa," he said to his father riding at his side, "It isn't the same!"

Señor Seguin chuckled. "It is the same, Juan, but you are different."

The sound of barking dogs and screaming children soon awoke the lazy town from its afternoon *siesta*. The deserted street began to fill with curious people as the group rode past. Juan trotted his horse proudly, calling to various friends along the way. He saw his brother and sister near the main plaza. Puffs of dust from Chico's hooves filled the air as Juan raced the remaining distance to the *hacienda*. Juan slid from the saddle to grab his sister and swung her above his head and down, as he had seen his father do so often. Small Leonidas laughed when she slipped and fell on her bottom. Her older brother helped her to her feet and hugged his brother Tomás.

"It is good to be home," Juan exclaimed happily and turned toward the doorway. His mother stood watching him. He raced to her side and kissed her cheek. *"Mamacita,* we are home! We are home!"

Señora Seguin looked up into her son's dark eyes and shook her head. "Juanito, you have grown so much."

With the news of their return, the *hacienda* bustled into action but Juan escaped to the pasture behind the adobe buildings. He whistled loudly. La Reina raised her head and looked in his direction. She galloped to his side. Her colt was at her heels. "La Reina, La Reina," he muttered over and over as he stroked her head while Prince butted his shoulder. "Boy," Juan exclaimed, "You have grown a foot." The mare whinnied softly.

The visitors settled into a routine. During the daylight hours they were in conference with Governor Martinez. Their evenings were filled with entertainment as prominent families took turns having them to their homes. The last night was reserved for the Seguins' *fiesta*.

Before daybreak the morning of the party, the women were busy grinding corn for tortillas and tamales. Huge pots of beans, spiced with hot chili peppers cooked over the outdoor wood fires. By afternoon the pungent aroma of freshly killed deer and goat roasting over charcoal fires filled the warm air. At dusk the guests began to arrive. Patio tables were laden with delicacies and the garden was decorated with colorful flowers.

Juan stood in the shadows. Dressed in tight fitting silver-trimmed pants and short jacket of midnight blue, he watched the people. How festive they looked in their brightly colored clothes. Graceful ladies dressed in ruffled, elaborate gowns that swished as they walked by.

As each family arrived they were introduced to the visitors: Governor and Señora Martinez, Juan Veramendi and his wife, the Antonio Navarros, and the José Flores family. At the mention of José Flores, Juan's heart skipped a beat. For one moment his eyes met those of his childhood friend, Gertrudis Flores. Like many of Spanish aristocracy ancestors, fourteen-year-old Gertrudis was tall and willowy. Her jet black hair was styled low on her regal neck to compliment her almond shaped black eyes. Juan understood and agreed to his father's wish that the two neighboring families would someday be united with his marriage to Gertrudis.

Feeling awkward and shy, Juan was content to remain in the background as the adults talked and visited.

The party lasted late into the night. Music from a string band played until the last visitor departed.

The next day all of San Antonio turned out to bid the Americans farewell. Juan, with the Baron's help, had learned a few words of English. "Go with God, until we meet again, Señor Austin."

Stephen Austin clasped his hand firmly and replied, "*Vaya usted con Dios,* Juan."

As the Americans rode away Juan waved his hat and cried, "*Adios,* good-bye. *Adios.*" The citizens watched the riders until they disappeared over the hills to the east. Juan wondered if his life would ever be the same after the trip to Nacogdoches, but it was not long until their household settled down into its easy ways again.

Often, after that, in the hot summer evenings Juan would go with his father to visit neighbors. He listened to the men and knew things were changing. After a bloody struggle in 1821, Mexico had won her freedom from Spain.

Don Erasmos listened to talk about Mexico with deep concern. More and more the name, Santa Anna, came into a conversation. When the Spanish tried to reinvade Mexico in 1824, Santa Anna and his army stopped them. After that Santa Anna called himself, the "Napoleon of the West." It was not long before he had taken over the government, and made himself President General of Mexico. He began at once to enlist a strong army to stamp out any opposition from the Mexican people.

With the passing of time, Juan grew into an outspoken young man with a determined look in his eyes. When Don Erasmos was appointed to the office of postmaster, Juan took over his father's duties on the rancho. He became a regular Sunday visitor at José Flores's ranch in hopes of seeing the beautiful Gertrudis.

One Sunday afternoon following his nineteenth

birthday, Juan dressed with extra care in his best and saddled La Reina to visit his neighbors. For days he had rehearsed his proposal speech, so, with an air of confidence, he asked Señor Flores for his daughter's hand in marriage. He was happy when Señor Flores agreed, and preparations for the wedding began.

Their whirlwind courtship and marriage was like a dream. On January 18th, 1826, Juan began a new life with his bride. They made a striking couple: Gertrudis's delicate Spanish beauty complimented Juan's distinguished appearance.

After their marriage, Juan became bold and sure of himself, like his father. More and more they opposed the Mexican leader, Antonio López de Santa Anna and his rise in power. As important citizens of San Antonio, the Seguins spoke out for liberty and independence to their fellow Mexican friends called *Tejanos*. Many of the ranchers and citizens agreed with them.

Life in other areas of Texas changed, too. Many Americans settlers had been given land grants to start settlements. Among them were Gonzales, Goliad, and Washington-on-the-Brazos.

One of the Americans was tall, handsome Jim Bowie. Searching for land and the legendary lost gold mine, he found his way to San Antonio. Jim Bowie saw Ursula Vermendi, the beautiful daughter of the wealthiest man in San Antonio, and lost his heart. Their romantic courtship and marriage brought Bowie's acceptance in the Mexican settlement. Stories of the Bowie knife worn in his belt gained him immediate respect from all.

Juan discovered that Bowie shared his own appreciation for horses and honesty. Gradually, a warm friendship developed between the two. He also discovered his new friend could speak several languages. Juan became fluent in English with Bowie's help. Later, he often translated in both languages.

The settlers lived peacefully as Mexican citizens, but marauding bands of hostile Indians were a constant threat. The small town of Gonzales was given a small cannon after the settlers asked the government for protection. Later, Santa Anna changed his mind about the cannon and sent soldiers to take it back. The settlers refused to surrender the cannon, and a small discussion followed. After that, the Texans began to talk of freedom. When Santa Anna heard about it he sent General Cos to San Antonio to defend the town against the would-be freedom fighters.

A small force, including Stephen Austin, Jim Bowie and Juan Seguin, met together to make plans. One of the first things they did was select Austin as their leader. He dispatched Juan's newly formed group to scout the area. With the coming of darkness, they decided to spend the night in the church of Concepcion.

Juan yawned and stretched. He realized again how quickly the years had flown and how his life was slipping by. At twenty-nine he was now father of four: Antonio six, José five, Josefa four, and little Juan two.

With a deep sign, Juan settled back on the hard dirt floor of the old mission. He wondered what tomorrow would bring for the other Texans asleep beside him. He knew General Cos's army was less than two miles away: would it mean victory or death for the freedom fighters?

2

The Battle For
San Antonio

BOOM!

The roar of the cannon shook the silence.

"Men, grab your rifles," Juan Seguin shouted. His voice echoed against the thick walls of the old church. "Sounds like Cos and his men are out there with a cannon. Let's show him how *Tejanos* fight. The cannon and victory!"

Ninety voices echoed that call through the foggy, misty October morning in 1835. The group, part of Stephen Austin's larger force, had awakened to find the mission surrounded by 400 Mexican soldiers. They poked their muskets through firing holes in the thick walls. Those holes had originally been put there for protection against an Indian attack, but Juan's men used them to their advantage. Over an open area the fog lifted to disclose the Mexican cannon turned in their direction. Each time a soldier attempted to fire the cannon, — a Texan aimed and pulled the trigger. One after another the cannoneers fell to the ground. Finally, the Mexican soldiers decided their efforts were useless. They turned and ran toward a clump of bushes in the distance.

"Bowie," Juan shouted. "They're moving back to the river."

Jim Bowie answered, "Load up, boys, let's take that cannon. But keep under cover, we haven't a man to spare."

Pausing long enough to reload, they rushed through the small rooms off the chapel, down the archway and past the well in the courtyard. Juan and his volunteers raced to the cannon, turned it toward the retreating army and lit the fuse. The sound filled the silence.

"Come on," Juan called. "They're on the run, let's keep after them."

The fog thickened as they approached the river bank. It was difficult to distinguish friend from foe.

Bowie shouted through the mist, "Hold your fire! No need wasting bullets or hitting one of our men by mistake. Those fellows are probably back to San Antonio by now the way they were running. Let's return to the churchyard."

"Guess we showed them," someone shouted.

"Sure did," a voice agreed.

In the murky light it was difficult to tell who had spoken. Most of the men in the newly formed unit didn't recognize each other by name or voice. But everyone knew Jim Bowie and Juan Seguin.

"Wonder how many we killed?" Bowie asked.

"Come on," Juan answered. "Let's gather the dead and wounded and find out."

Bowie agreed. One by one the casualties were carried to the yard. They did what they could to help the injured. Haze hung over the church's bell towers as they looked at the dead.

15

"I counted sixty and one Texan. Anyone recognize him?" Bowie asked.

"That's Richard Andrews," Noah Smithwick said.

"Sixty! We only fought about thirty minutes and they outnumbered us four to one! We're going to win this war with Santa Anna for sure, won't we, Seguin?" someone yelled.

Juan nodded. "Come on, men, let's bury them and move on."

It did not take long to dig the graves in the soft dirt and bury the dead. "That's all we can do here, boys," Juan said. "Austin's waiting for us on the other side of the river near town. Let's go."

Sometime later the ninety rode to a cluster of adobe houses and deserted thatched huts about a mile from Juan's hacienda.

"Howdy, boys," Francis Johnson shouted to the men gathered around a fire in front of one of the shacks. "You're looking at heroes!"

"What happened?" someone demanded.

"We sent old General Cos running for cover in less than thirty minutes! And we killed sixty of his men," Noah Smithwick bragged as they slid from their horses.

Stephen Austin had stood silently listening, his face was grave. "How many did you lose?"

"Only one, sir," Juan replied.

Hearing that news the men gave a victory shout.

"Good work, boys," Austin exclaimed. He broke into a hacking cough that shook his frail body. Juan Seguin felt compassion and concern for his longtime friend. In 1833, Austin had gone to Mexico to ask Santa Anna for statehood for Texas. The President General answered the request by putting him under arrest and keeping him in prison for almost two years. Juan watched his friend's pale face. He looked much older than his forty-two years; the months in prison had broken his health.

"We are going to force Cos to surrender by cutting off his reinforcements and waiting him out. When he's hungry he'll give up," Austin explained.

"Sir," Juan declared, "I think we should attack now."

"Why?"

"Look at our men. Most of them aren't dressed for a long winter siege, Stephen," Juan replied. "Some are wearing buckskin breeches already hard and black from rain and dirt; they'll freeze when it gets cold. Few of them have boots, and most have shoes or moccasins that give little protection."

"I agree," Francis Johnson joined in. "Sick men can't fight."

Jim Bowie got into the discussion. "We haven't much to eat even if we do shoot rabbits and squirrels. We'll starve if Seguin and his volunteers can't sneak into town for food. Good thing we have friends there or we'd have no corn and beans or coffee. Austin, admit it. This is a ragtag army!" Bowie shook his head in disgust. "I say attack now! It's foolish to wait."

Juan spoke up for the men. "We may look ragtag, Jim, but we can fight. Don't forget that!" From the expression on Austin's face, they knew further discussion was useless.

The men grumbled and complained amongst themselves in the weeks that followed because the days grew colder with the coming of winter. In spite of Juan's friends and their gifts of beans and coffee, rations were in short supply. They took turns in hunting for food, but each morning the number of Texans grew smaller. The volunteer army was free to come and go. Some became discouraged with the cold weather and lack of activity.

Many returned to their families and the warmth of their homes.

On the morning of November 15th, a horse and rider galloped into camp. Some of the men recognized him.

"Howdy, Burleson," one of them called.

The Indian fighter rode to the center of the group, dismounted and looked around. "Where's Stephen Austin?"

"Here I am."

"Edward Burleson reporting, sir."

"Good to have you. Men, get Burleson some coffee and take his horse." He turned to face the newcomer. "What is new?"

"Guess you know that the delegates have been meeting in San Felipe to decide what to do," Burleson replied between sips of coffee.

"And?" Austin waited.

"That's why I'm here, I've come to help command. Here's a letter for you from Sam Houston. He has been elected major general of the Texas army."

A murmur of approval went through the group.

"Good man, Houston," Johnson remarked.

"Shhh, let's listen," someone muttered.

Burleson removed a letter from the pocket of his deerskin coat and handed it to Stephen Austin. "You are to go to the United States."

Austin read the report. His face was set in a frown when he turned and announced loudly for all to hear: "Burleson is your new commander, Francis Johnson is next in line. I must leave at once."

"Why, Stephen? Can't I go? You're half sick with that cough," Juan declared.

"Thanks, Seguin, but I have to go to Washington, to appeal for money and volunteers to fight. Houston promoted you to temporary captain." He broke into a cough, his face was flushed with fever. "Would one of you get my horse?"

Austin turned to his makeshift headquarters in the adobe hut to gather his personal belongings. Noah Smithwick and Juan saddled the horse. A hush fell over the Texans as Austin tied his bedroll behind his saddle and turned to them.

"We do not know what is ahead but I know you will do your best."

With a quick salute, Stephen Austin mounted, and without a backward glance, rode to the east away from San Antonio.

A cold wind blew from the north. A fine drizzle began to fall.

Silently, the Texans moved into the shacks to escape the November chill.

The days that followed were filled with discontentment. Each morning when Burleson attempted to drill the men he found their morale and enthusiasm at a low ebb. He knew Ben Milam, Johnson and others were restless. The men grumbled and complained because they wanted to attack and fight.

The morning of December 4th broke with excitement. Hearing the noise, Burleson walked from his quarters. "What is it?" he demanded.

"Sir," Seguin explained from near the fire. "This man is a deserter from General Cos's army. He tells me that Cos's men are cold and hungry, too. They killed some of their horses for food!"

The Texans listened with disgust. But it was possible they might get that hungry.

"This is a good time to attack," Johnson cried in a forceful voice. "We've waited long enough!"

"That's right," one of the men grumbled. "Let's fight!"

"But," Burleson shouted above the confusion, "You forget, I'm in charge here! I say we wait!" He thrust his hands in his pockets and turned on his heel to stalk to his quarters.

The group sat around the fire protesting and arguing about what they should do. The morning was tense; a feeling of expectancy filled the air as the men cleaned their rifles.

In the middle of the afternoon confusion again erupted. Three Texas volunteers who had been Cos's prisoners ran into camp. Everyone started talking and asking questions at the same time.

"What happened?" a voice boomed from the back of the crowd.

"How did you fellows get away from Cos?" someone demanded.

Juan Seguin stepped forward and raised his hand. Gradually a hush fell on the unit. He cleared his throat and asked, "What did happen?" He looked from one man to another.

The oldest of the three replied, "Seguin, you remember me? I'm Sam Maverick and that's John W. Smith. Well, you asked how we got here — we escaped! Cos's men are so disgusted and hungry they let us go!"

The Texans gave a mighty shout.

"Couldn't happen to a better bunch!" a man cried.

Ben Milam stepped to Juan's side. His eyes flashed and he declared with a roar. "Boys, I've done a heap of fighting in my forty-seven years and I've been in more than one Mexican prison during this squabble for freedom. I don't know about you, but I'm tired of waiting, and I say let's attack!"

"We're with you, Milam," Johnson boomed.

"Who will go with old Ben Milam into San Antonio?"

Milam drew a line on the ground with the heel of his boot. "Who will follow old Ben Milam?"

The men jumped over the line with a mighty cheer. Burleson stood at the edge of the circle, his face clouded with anger.

"This is your town," Ben said turning to Juan. "How do you figure we should make our surprise attack?"

All eyes turned to Juan Seguin. He rubbed his chin and thought a moment before replying. "We have about three hundred men. If they were in two groups we could surround the plaza to get to those cannons."

"Good idea," Milam nodded. "Then what?"

"Then we could fight from house to house and chase them back to the Alamo."

"Sounds good to me. What do you think, James Neill?"

Neill nodded. "Might work."

Milam turned to the men on his left. "You fellows over there will come with me." He looked to the right. "You all go with Johnson. Where will we start?"

Juan pushed the black hair from his eyes before answering. "We'll have to be careful. Cos has soldiers on the rooftops. We could use the De La Garza and Veramendi houses for cover. They're deserted."

Before dawn the next morning, December 5th, the Texans were ready. Milam moved to the front of his group and Johnson to his. "Let's go, boys," Milam ordered. "But keep it quiet. Don't shoot until you have to. Surprise is our best defense."

The first rays of light were coming into the sky as they crept silently toward two vacant houses.

Suddenly, voices shouted from one of the rooftops, *"Mire! Mire!"* "Look, Look!"

The sound of muskets and cannon soon filled the crisp air. Milam's column, armed with crowbars and bat-

21

tering rams, moved from room to room in the De La
Garza house. Johnson's unit forced its way through the
Veramendi doors. Once inside, the Texans settled down
for battle.

All that day and the next, the 6th, the 300 Texans
fought against staggering odds but one enemy soldier
after another fell to the ground.

Near dark on the second day, Milam's orders were
passed among the men. "After dark we're to dig a trench
out there in the Veramendi yard. That way we'll have
protection yet can make our bullets count."

Later, under the cloak of night, they dug a ditch
using the crowbars and their hands in place of shovels.

Early the next morning the fighting resumed. The
cool air was soon thick again with gunpowder and smoke.

Musket answered rifle blast. Ben Milam stood by
the new barricade. He raised his hand to give an order.
"Men — "

A sniper on a nearby rooftop had seen Milam. He
aimed and fired. The bullet hit Ben in the forehead, spin-
ning him around. He slumped to the ground between
Juan Seguin and Sam Maverick.

Juan bent down to feel his pulse and shook his head.
"They've killed Ben Milam. He's dead!"

Word spread like wildfire. "They hit Ben!"
Seguin cried, "Texas for Texans, come on!"

With that battle cry they fought like wildcats. Mexican soldier after soldier fell in his tracks as they were
chased through the streets. The Texans moved from one
house to another.

Johnson yelled, "They're retreating to the Alamo!
We've got them in a panic, keep it up!"

With a mighty yell they doubled their efforts.

"Men!" shouted Seguin. "Look! Cos has deserted

22

those cannons. Some of you give me a hand. Let's turn them around toward the Alamo."

Several ran forward to help push and shove the cannons into place. The cannons were soon loaded and readied for firing. Again and again they fired the cannon. The air was thick with smoky haze. Finally, with the coming of night, the bombardment stopped. Silence came to the small town.

During the morning of the fifth day, a lull fell over the Alamo. Juan raised his hand and shouted, "Hold your fire! Something's happening over there." An expectant hush fell over the group, they watched and waited.

"Look," Bowie cried. "A white flag! They're giving up!"

Edward Burleson, who had been in the back ranks, stepped forward. "Well! We've done it. I'll accept the surrender." He turned to Seguin. "Cos may not speak English and my Spanish isn't very good. Please, come and translate."

They met the General in the cleared area in front of the Alamo.

Cos was the first to speak. "I, General Martin Perfecto de Cos — surrender!"

The officer's brightly colored uniform, bedecked with shiny medals and ribbons, looked conspicuous beside the buckskins worn by the Texans.

"I, Edward Burleson, accept your surrender. How many men do you have?" He waited for Juan to repeat the question in Spanish.

Cos replied, "I have one thousand and one hundred."

Burleson scratched his head and wondered what to do with so many prisoners. Finally, he decided there was only one thing he could do, send them back to Mexico. He said, "Tell him the conditions of his surrender: he will be allowed to return to his country if he pledges he will never fight in Texas again." Burleson paused and added in a more confidential voice. "Seguin, you and your volunteers will go with William Travis to follow them to the Rio Grande River. Keep an eye out along the way for stray horses. We could use them."

Burleson listened to the rapid fire exchange of words between Juan and the General. "Sir," Juan explained in English. "He is afraid of Indians and demands we give him protection."

"All right," Burleson grumbled. "We'll give them just enough weapons and powder in case there's an attack, but you be sure they leave Texas without them."

The Texans were wild with excitement over their victory. Outnumbered four to one, they had won and could head homeward.

The next day many, including Burleson, started home to their families to celebrate Christmas and settled down to farm life again. With Cos and his army on the way back to Mexico they thought the fighting was all over. Unfortunately, their joy was to be short-lived.

Juan Seguin, with William Travis and the volunteers, started marching the soldiers to the south. The 150 mile trip to the Rio Grande River was hard on the Texans and the Mexicans. The weather was miserable. A cold north wind, and icy showers slowed their journey.

Finally, after a number of days, the weary group approached the border — the river that separated Mexico from Texas.

"Everyone off your horses," Juan shouted in Spanish. "Cos, you and your aides move forward." The soldiers obeyed. Suddenly, on a signal from Juan, the volunteers yelled and began firing their rifles into the air, causing the horses to stampede in the opposite direction. Without weapons, there was little the Mexican soldiers could do but watch their horses disappear in the direction they had just traveled.

"*Adios, amigos,*" one of Seguin's men cried as they rode off after the horses. Cos and his soldiers shook their fists and protested bitterly as they waded into the cold river to turn south toward Saltillo, Mexico.

3

Messenger Of the Alamo

The first weeks of 1836 were dismal. Cold blasts of north wind brought a steady downpour of rain. Juan felt an ominous cloak of gloom had settled over San Antonio when he and his men rode into town. He soon learned the reason. Sam Houston had sent Jim Bowie and his thirty friends with instructions for James Neill to blow up the Alamo! But, after much discussion, James Neill had given up his command. William Travis had taken charge. Instead of being destroyed, the Alamo, under the command of both Travis and Bowie, was now being fortified for battle.

Rumors from Mexico warned that Santa Anna was preparing to march against the rebels. Many Mexican citizens of San Antonio were worried; they were caught in the middle. They didn't agree with the Texans, and were afraid of the President General of Mexico.

Juan sympathized with his Mexican friends. He was

relieved he had sent word for his family to leave the ranch and move to Nacogdoches, before trouble started.

Later, approaching the winding river, Juan looked at the old church in the distance. The Alamo, founded in 1718 by the Franciscan priests for a mission to teach the Indians, had been in disuse for years. Parts of the roof had collapsed but the thick stone walls were sturdy. The twelve-foot high stone wall surrounding most of the three-acre compound was still standing in spite of the attack the Texans had made before Cos surrendered.

Juan rode through the gate and stopped. He saw men attempting to patch the breaks in the north and south wall. Cannon that had been deserted by the Mexican soldiers were being repaired and readied for firing. Juan slid from his saddle and whispered into the horse's ear, "Prince, looks like you'll get a chance to rest for awhile." He walked him to the corral and unsaddled the horse.

In the days that followed, Juan wondered how anyone could hope to make a fortress out of the building. After Cos's surrender, the Alamo had been stripped of guns, blankets and ammunition. There was little of use. Juan wondered if a well-equipped army couldn't defend those walls, how could a handful of Texans?

But February 8th brought a ray of hope to the fort; famous frontiersman Davy Crockett and twelve companions rode into town. Juan learned later that Santa Anna's main army had reached the Rio Grande that same day.

After Crockett's arrival the men celebrated for a week with races, dances, speeches and rejoicing. No one dreamed Santa Anna's forces could be marching closer while Davy fiddled on his violin. Scotsman John McGregor added to the noise with his bagpipes. On a suggestion from Juan, a sentry was posted on the roof of the highest point in the city, San Fernando Church.

At daybreak on February 23rd, after a noisy night of

27

dancing and singing, the drowsy watchman in the church tower yawned and peered at the horizon. Shivering from the morning chill, he looked to the east and stretched. Then he gazed to the south and then the west. Suddenly he gasped and blinked. He rubbed his eyes and looked again. Seizing the bell rope, he pulled and pulled with all his strength. His eyes were glued on hundreds of horses and men marching toward the sleeping town.

With the pealing of the warning bell, panic broke loose in the streets. People, in various stages of undress, ran from their houses. Travis shouted over the racket, "Everyone move inside the Alamo."

"The enemy is upon us!" one man shouted.

A woman screamed and dashed into her house. Soon families, loaded with all they could carry, were scurrying out of town as fast as they could go. A few who sympathized with the Texans hurried to the compound walls of the mission. Some braver souls decided to lock their doors and ignore the confusion.

Some men, women and children flooded into the Alamo for protection. Colonel Travis attempted to organize his forces. "Crockett, have those men close that south gate and get those families somewhere so they'll be safe." One by one the men found a place to serve.

Later, the Colonel dispatched Dr. John Sutherland and John Smith to Goliad and Gonzales with a message for James Fannin. In his letter he stated they would fire a cannon at dawn, noon, and sunset to let the outside world know they were still fighting.

Travis counted his troops and stationed the 150 fighters along the rectangular area of the churchyard. Crockett and his twelve sharpshooters were assigned to the weakest spot along the south wall.

Volunteers searched the area around the Alamo for food supplies. They returned a short time later with eighty sacks of corn and thirty steers. The steers were placed in the cattlepen on the east wall.

That afternoon Santa Anna's army took possession of the town of San Antonio. After a brief exchange of messages between Travis and the Mexican General, a red flag of "no quarter" was unfurled over San Fernando church. It would be a fight to the death — no prisoners would be taken.

About a half mile away, at the Alamo, the high spirited Texans prepared for battle. Cannons were moved into place for firing; rifles and muskets were cleaned and loaded.

Juan and others were securing a cannon on a dirt platform in the center of the yard when Juan looked in Jim Bowie's direction. He saw him stagger and collapse. Juan blinked and burst into action. "Give me a hand, boys," he yelled as he raced to Bowie's side. The stricken man was carried into a room and placed on a cot. "Get the doctor," Juan ordered. "He's burning with fever!"

One of the men dashed from the room yelling, "Where's Doctor Pollard? Bowie needs him."

Doctor Amos Pollard heard his name and hurried forward. "Where?"

"In there," he pointed to the door of the small room.

Once inside, the doctor's experienced hands examined the patient. Finally, he looked up and shook his head. "Pneumonia and complete exhaustion! He needs rest."

Bowie's lashes fluttered, his eyes opened. "Travis," he mumbled. ". . . Get Travis." His thin body shook with a hacking cough.

Juan clasped his battered sombrero and waited silently at the foot of the bed. His forty-year-old friend's grief-stricken face was gaunt and pale. He had watched Bowie's zest for life dwindle since his wife and children

29

had died from cholera several years earlier. Juan knew Bowie might be sick of pneumonia but heartache and loneliness were the cause.

Travis entered the darkened room and looked around. He saw the men standing along the wall. "You fellows go about your work. Seguin, you stay with the doctor." Travis waited for the others to leave, then cleared his throat. "Sorry to hear you're sick, Bowie."

"I'm giving up my command," Bowie whispered hoarsely. "You have complete control." He coughed violently, then continued. "Tell my men, Juan. Good luck. You'll need it." He sank back upon the bed exhausted.

Colonel William Travis looked at Jim Bowie and shook his head. Running his fingers thoughtfully through his red hair, he sighed.

With the first rays of light on February 24th, the Mexican cannons began their bombardment. The air grew thick with gunpowder and smoke. The shelling stopped to start again and stop.

Between attacks the Texans repaired the damage done to their defenses. Sentries watched toward the east for reinforcements. They did not come.

Inside the chapel were the wives and children. Captain Almeron Dickinson's wife, Susanna, and daughter were among the families. During the heavy bombardment the mothers knelt to pray and tried to soothe their frightened children. In the brief lulls between the fighting they cooked for the men.

With darkness, when the shooting died down, Davy Crockett and his men told stories and joked around the campfires. Often Davy played his fiddle and sang.

One day slipped into another as fighting continued but ammunition began to dwindle. In the black moonless nights, Santa Anna's army of thousands tightened its grasp like a giant vise until the Alamo was encircled on all four sides. There was no way to escape.

On the evening of February 29th, after six days of fighting, Colonel Travis called a meeting of his officers. One by one the men, including Juan Seguin, gathered around Travis's headquarters and waited. Their faces showed the strain of battle from the constant bombardment and lack of sleep.

"Men," Travis said, looking from one to another. "We must get help and reinforcements. There has been no answer to the dispatches sent to Fannin. I have written another. The question is, who will go?" He paused. "You realize, of course, the danger of crossing the enemy lines. We are surrounded. Anyone want to volunteer?" He looked from Crockett to Dickinson on around the room.

No one spoke.

Captain Juan Seguin stepped forward. All eyes rested on him. "Sir, I will go!"

Travis protested, "But, Seguin, I need you."

"Sir, I think I am the only one who could get through those sentries. Being a *Tejano,* I could answer in Spanish if a soldier stopped me. I could pretend to be one of them." Travis shook his head. "I don't like it, but let's take a vote." The majority voted in favor of Juan Sequin being the messenger. Travis reluctantly agreed. "Besides, I'll be able to find my way in the dark, I know this country." "Colonel, I don't have a horse." Seguin paused to swallow the lump that formed in his throat with the thought of his Prince. "My horse was killed in one of their attacks. I'll ask Bowie if I can borrow his."

Travis nodded, rumpling his hair with his fingers. "Guess you are right, Seguin." He sighed. "Had hoped to use you if Santa Anna sent a message but this dispatch must get out of here. Better take one of your men with you." He handed Juan a paper from his desk. "Give this

31

to Fannin. Tell him we must have help or — " He did not finish.

"Sir," Juan replied as he folded the message and put it in his pocket. "I'll take Antonio Oroche with me. But if we wait until it's dark and they've settled for the night, we'll have a better chance of getting through."

The Colonel sighed and agreed. "You're probably right. When you come back you'll hear a rifle shot every hour on the hour as a signal if we are still fighting. "Well," he paused, "good luck, Seguin. Our future rests on that message getting out so we can have reinforcements."

"I'll do my best, sir," Juan said and looked to his friends who shook his hand. "Good luck to you, *amigos. Vaya usted con Dios.*" With a quick salute, Juan smashed his hat on his head and turned on his heels to walk out into the dusky evening. Drops of rain and a sharp north wind hit his face.

Later, in the hushed blackness, Juan and his aide silently slipped out the north gate. A short distance away from the gate a Mexican cavalry patrol had dismounted to rest and graze their horses. The two *Tejanos* rode slowly forward, talking in Spanish. The patrols, thinking them part of their own group, were unconcerned. Suddenly, Juan and Antonio spurred their horses, leaning over their necks to avoid being shot in case of an attack. The soldiers, realizing they'd been tricked, reached for their guns. Bullets whizzed by the riders. They dashed toward a grove of trees to disappear before the enemy could mount and give chase in the night.

The two riders raced on. Mile after mile slid under the horses' hooves. The two men clasped their *serapes* tightly for protection from the steady drizzle. Finally, satisfied they were not being pursued, Juan slowed his horse.

"We'll rest here, Antonio. We can't make the ninety miles to Goliad without stopping." They hobbled the horses and tied them to a low bush near a patch of grass. "Let's build a fire, I'm cold." After gathering wood, Juan discovered, to his disgust, it was too wet to burn. They huddled near a tree for shelter from the wind.

Dawn was breaking as they started out again. "We'll get something to eat at San Bartolo ranch on the other side of Cibolo Creek," Juan explained as the sun's rays filled the eastern sky.

"*Bueno,* I'm hungry."

A short time later, they rode up over a small hill. Up ahead something moved. As they rode closer they saw a man herding cows across a narrow ravine. With their guns cocked, they approached the bearded rider. Juan lowered his rifle and exclaimed in surprise, "Those cows have our brand on them!"

With a crooked smile the man replied, "Really? Then you must be Seguin. I'm Captain Desauque. Fannin sent me to your ranch for food for our men."

Juan nodded with a frown on his face. "I'm Juan Seguin, but where is Fannin? I have a message for him from Colonel Travis. He could use that food and some help, or hasn't Fannin heard? Santa Anna's surrounded the Alamo!"

Desauque answered. "Fannin knows. We started out for San Antonio but the wagons broke down. Fannin had us turn back!"

"Turn back?" Seguin stared in disbelief. "Isn't Fannin sending help?"

"Well," Desauque rubbed his chin thoughtfully and replied. "He should be here in a day or two."

"A day or two? Doesn't he know the lives of those men at the Alamo depend on him?" Juan clinched his fist around the horse's reins and spit out his words. "You ride to Fannin and tell him that. Tell him I'm waiting here until he sends reinforcements. Give him this message from Travis." Juan took the dispatch from his pocket and watched the man place it in his saddlebag. "Travis must have men . . . and soon!"

The captain wheeled his horse around and yelled back over his shoulder, "I'll tell him."

Seguin's face wrinkled in a frown. "Wish those steers were going to Travis instead of Fannin."

Sometime later a messenger brought Fannin's reply. A young, smooth-shaven man galloped up to the fire and said, "You must be Captain Seguin."

Juan replied, "Yes, I'm Seguin."

"I'm Lieutenant Finley. Colonel Fannin sent me to tell you there has been a change in his plans. He started out but received word that General Urrea is preparing to attack Goliad so he turned back!"

"Turned back?" Antonio moaned.

"Yes, Fannin says for you to go to Gonzales for reinforcements. General Houston's forming a unit there."

Juan stared blankly up at the messenger. "You mean Fannin isn't sending anyone?"

"That's right, sir. Sorry. In fact, I have orders to return as soon as I deliver this message to you." He lifted his hand for a half-hearted salute and turned his horse toward Goliad.

They stood watching the man until he disappeared behind the oak trees. Antonio looked disgusted. "That settles that. Now what?"

Picking up his gear to saddle his horse, Juan replied, "We ride to General Houston. We've wasted too much time on Fannin as it is."

Later in the day Juan and Antonio rode into the camp at Gonzales. The tantalizing aroma of boiling coffee and broiling beef welcomed them along with greetings from the men.

"*Buenos dias,* Seguin," Salvador Flores called. "Thought you were at the Alamo, what happened? You look tired; come get something to eat and tell us the news."

Slipping from their horses the two moved toward the fire. Juan asked, "Where's Houston?"

"We expect him any minute, sir. He's helping the delegates at Washington-on-the-Brazos draw up a Texas Declaration of Independence." Salvador filled two metal cups with coffee from a pot and handed them to the newcomers. "Captain, you will see most of our Ninth company here waiting for orders."

Juan looked around the camp, nodding to various men in the circle that had formed around them. "Guess the only ones not here are the seven I left at the Alamo."

One of the men stepped forward and asked, "Is it true Santa Anna has the Alamo surrounded?"

"It's true all right," Seguin declared. "We were lucky to get out, but we'll get back in somehow. Things look bad. Travis needs ammunition and reinforcements, that's why we're here."

"You must have just missed the thirty-two from Gonzales," Salvador said.

"We didn't see them," Antonio remarked. "They'll help some."

Andrea Barcena spoke up, "Sir, things aren't good here either. Indians are attacking the nearby settlements, the people are afraid. And Santa Anna's scouts have been stealing their cattle, everyone is nervous."

"Glad you and Antonio came, Captain Seguin," Manuel Orche joined in. "We need a leader, no one knows what to do without Houston."

They grumbled and complained about the lack of organization until after dark.

The next morning they awoke to the news, "Houston's here!"

The camp sprang into motion. The General ordered various ones to assume certain duties.

Juan reported to his Commander-of-the-Army. "Sir, I'm Juan Seguin from San Antonio. Colonel Travis sent me with a message for Fannin in Goliad, but Fannin can't help. Travis needs reinforcements. Understand Gonzales sent thirty-two men before we arrived, but that will only bring the number at the Alamo to about one hundred and eighty-six or so. Travis needs at least two hundred to defend those walls and he needs provisions."

Houston nodded. "Captain, take part of your second regiment and wait for further orders on the road outside San Antonio. You can leave when you're ready. Meanwhile, I'm sending Flores and twenty-five of your company to protect the ranches."

After that Juan and his men lost no time riding to the assigned location to wait for instructions. Finally additional men and supplies arrived, along with orders for them to proceed to the Alamo.

As they prepared to leave Juan's face was grim. "Hope we're not too late, today's March the sixth."

The group arrived at Cibolo Creek. Juan raised his hand and said, "Listen." The group heard no sounds coming from the direction of San Antonio. Nothing. Antonio slipped from his saddle to place his ear on the ground. After a few minutes he stood and shook his head. Nothing.

Suddenly one of the men pointed toward the town and cried, "Look!"

The sun's rays cast ghostly shadows over the western horizon as great billows of black smoke floated into the sky.

"Something's burning," Antonio yelled.

Captain Seguin rubbed his chin thoughtfully. "I don't know what that means. Vergara, you and Barcena ride forward and scout around. We'll wait here until sunset and start back. General Houston's orders were for us to return if there was no signal from Travis."

The two scouts rode toward the fort. Juan looked at the horses behind him that were loaded with supplies. "We don't want these to fall into Santa Anna's hands." The sun was sinking in the west when Juan called to his volunteers, "Boys, come on! Let's head back to Gonzales."

After dark they stopped to rest the horses. The two scouts overtook them. "Captain," Vergara said, "Looks like the Alamo has fallen!"

"Are you sure?"

Barcena nodded his head. "Yes, we met a fellow who told us that smoke we saw was Santa Anna burning the dead!"

"You mean all of the men at the Alamo are dead?"

Vergara spoke up, "That's what we were told."

The small group remounted and rode in silence, each thinking his own thoughts. Juan was remembering his friends: Jim Bowie, William Travis, Almeron Dickinson and the others. His heart was heavy.

A short time after they rejoined the main force in Gonzales, "Deaf" Smith rode into camp cradling a child in his arms. Juan recognized Mrs. Susanna Dickinson riding behind Smith. He rushed to her side. "Mrs. Dickinson, how did you get here?"

She sighed wearily. "Santa Anna let me go. I have a letter for General Houston."

"Someone get the General," Juan ordered while he helped her from her horse.

Houston stepped from his tent a short distance away. "Someone call me?"

"Sir," Juan explained from near the fire. "This is Captain Almeron Dickinson's wife. She has a message from San Antonio."

A small circle of curious soldiers gathered around them to listen. All eyes were on the young lady as she said, "The Alamo has fallen! All are dead!"

"*All?*" the men echoed.

"All!" Tears of grief trickled down the woman's tired face. "Santa Anna sent you this, General." She handed him a paper.

Houston read it with a grim expression clouding his face. He looked from Mrs. Dickinson and her daughter to his soldiers. "Men! We're moving out! Santa Anna will give no quarter, no prisoners will be taken!"

"No prisoners?" they muttered.

"No prisoners!" Houston repeated as he turned to Juan. "Captain, have your men tie their bandanas around their heads so we'll recognize them as the rear guards. We can't leave the women and children, ride back to the settlement and order them to join us. Burn the houses, leave nothing for the enemy." He turned to his troops, "Start breaking camp. Move out!"

The men jumped into action. They saddled the horses, dismantled the tents then packed them onto the mules.

"Come on," Juan called to his company as he headed his horse toward Gonzales. With grim faces, they galloped from house to house echoing the warning, "Santa Anna's coming!"

"Get your things, move out! The enemy's heading this way!"

"Hurry! We have orders to burn everything. Move out!"

At first the women were confused, but the gloomy

looks of the men spurred them to start packing. Soon, the bewildered women had loaded all they could carry. They hurried into the night with their frightened children. The peaceful scene had changed to one of panic and fear. Tears for the dead at the Alamo were forgotten; the living had to think about themselves.

4

Fighting At San Jacinto

Panic filled the night. Houston's men began their retreat an hour before midnight that March 13th. The frightened women and children were close behind. They had traveled a short distance when the horizon turned golden red, giving the sky an eerie glow. In hushed silence the settlers looked back at their town. Muffled sobs and moans broke the stillness.

Suddenly, a woman screamed. "Willy! Where's my Willy?" Her voice rose to a crescendo. "My Willy! The baby's not here!"

Hands reached out to stop the woman as she started back. "Let me go!" she screamed. "Let me go! I'm going for my baby!"

Juan Seguin made his way through the mob, "Which house is yours?"

"The last one on the square," the mother sobbed. "I've got to —"

"You stay here, I'll go." Juan wheeled his horse

around before she could make a protest. The crowd moved aside to give him room to pass. He turned toward the rosy brightness of Gonzales. The horse whinnied in protest and fear. Juan slipped the bandana from his own head and bent forward in the saddle to place it on the eyes of the animal. Once the horse could no longer see the fire, he obeyed Juan's signals.

Sparks from the first fire spread through the grass to the nearest house and on to the next. Flames warmed the night, the thin oak boards burned quickly. Cinders from the adjoining homes were igniting the shingled roof of the last cabin when Juan jumped from his horse and tied him to a bush.

Juan raced for the open door into the smoke filled room. In the corner he could see a movement. As Juan raced to the frightened boy a dog at his feet barked and yelped to welcome him. Willy's arms flew around Juan's neck. "Mama, mama!" he cried hysterically.

Not to be left behind, the whining dog put his little paw on Juan's leg. Juan scooped him up and headed for the door with the dog in one arm and the child in the other. Racing from the burning building into the yard, he balanced the two while he untied the horse and leaped into the saddle. Flames ate at the wooden structure as they galloped away.

Riding back to rejoin the group, Juan felt relieved to know his own family was safe from danger. The refugees saw them coming and cheered, "Hurrah for Juan Seguin!"

The mother took her baby in her arms. "Willy, Willy," she sobbed. Clasping the child to her breast she looked up at Juan crying, "Thank you, thank you!" She joined the bewildered mob to move onward in the darkness.

On and on they walked. Minutes passed into hours, time lost its meaning. In the early dawn rain began to fall. The wet, dismal group crept toward the east. Horses headed the procession, then foot soldiers. Next came the women and children followed by Juan's company. The road became muddy and difficult as the rains continued.

Hour upon hour they marched, pausing only long enough to eat and rest. It was reported that Santa Anna's forces were getting closer. The trail became clogged with treasured possessions abandoned along the way.

Mile after mile of slick, soggy ground passed under their feet. Day gave way to night and night to day. One lapsed into another. With the passing of time, food grew scarce. Too exhausted to cry, the hungry travelers were cold and miserable. Mud spattered their clothing and clung to their shoes. Children cried and complained. Grim faced and forlorn, they rested along the way, then started again. Sheets of rain continued to beat upon the weary band.

Rumors passed up and down the lines. "Houston's taking us to the border of Louisiana!"

"Someone said we're heading for the Gulf of Mexico. Why don't we stop and fight?"

"Did you hear? Santa Anna's right behind us!"

Juan tried to calm their fears. "Don't be afraid. General Houston knows what he's doing. He just isn't talking."

Finally, they camped at a plantation on the west bank of the Brazos River. Juan's volunteers found corn in an abandoned crib and some cows in a pasture. The women and children looked for branches and twigs to burn. The men managed to start fires with the wet wood. A warm blaze encouraged the bedraggled group and they cooked the freshly killed meat.

For a short time the clouds parted to let the sunshine through. General Houston kept the men busy cleaning their guns, organizing a medical corps and cutting a trail in the dense grove of trees to the east.

The clouds returned and dumped their contents upon

the muddy earth. News of the massacre of James Fannin and his three hundred men at Goliad spread like a blanket of gloom over the camp.

"Anyone hear what happened?" a voice demanded.

"Understand Colonel Fannin thought his men would be treated with the honor due prisoners of war so he surrendered to General Urrea," was the reply.

"Then what?"

"A week later," someone answered, "Fannin and his troops were marched out on the prairie and shot!"

"Shot?"

"Massacred! Murdered!"

Word spread, men spoke in stunned whispers. Some deserted to join the families fleeing toward Louisiana. Others wanted to turn and fight the enemy.

Houston struggled to form the remaining 900 men into a fighting force. Some doubted Houston's courage and openly declared, "I think we need a new leader."

A gift of two cannon from the people of Cincinnati lifted their spirits momentarily, but the next morning they resumed their march. They moved east to the marshy San Jacinto River basin. Behind them were the thick woods of the Buffalo Bayou. Late the evening of April 19th, Deaf Smith rode into camp waving a saddle bag in his hand. "Look," he yelled. "I took this from a Mexican soldier!" He tossed the bag at Juan's feet, he picked it up and turned it over.

"General Houston," Juan shouted. "This has William Barret Travis's name on it."

The General moved forward and took the satchel. Opening it he removed a map along with various papers. Houston poured over them, they were the enemy's plan of attack. Sometime later he announced, "Men, Victory is certain! Trust in God and fear not!"

His words brought hope. "Remember the Alamo!" someone cried.

"Remember Goliad!" Voices echoed the cries.

Meanwhile, not far away in Santa Anna's camp, plans were being made to encircle the Texans. In the darkness they moved their camp closer to erect barricades and strengthen their position. All night they worked. In the early morning hours General Martin Perfecto de Cos arrived with more reinforcements. His 500 soldiers had marched for hours, they were tired. As the April sun rose higher over the marshy bayou, the humidity increased. The Mexican soldiers grew sleepier and sleepier. Finally, in the middle of the afternoon, they settled for a nap. The Mexican camp was silent.

In the meantime, the Texans watched an eagle soar overhead and loaded their guns. Juan Seguin talked with one after another of his Second Regiment volunteers. The bandanas on their heads served to identify them. Like the other Texans, their clothes were tattered and stiff with mud.

Colonel Thomas Rusk walked to Juan and stopped. "Did you see that eagle this morning, Seguin?" Juan nodded. "The General says that's a good luck sign!" The Colonel squinted one eye and smiled. "Do you like to fight?"

"Well," Juan chuckled, "I'm ready and willing to fight now."

The Colonel looked at the men gathered behind Juan. "It's three thirty. Let's go!"

That was the command they had been waiting for. The foot soldiers quickly formed a long thin line along the front of the woods.

"Ready? Forward!" That order was passed along.

"Hold your fire!" There was no sound but that of feet marching through the tall grass.

General Houston watched his troops from his white horse. When they were in position he waved his battered hat to signal attack.

BOOM! The cannon shattered the peaceful afternoon. Drummers and fifers had been placed along the line. They broke into the rousing song, *Will you Come to the Bower?* The fighting started.

The Texans sprang upon the enemy with wild cries of *Remember the Alamo! Remember Goliad!* They released their pent-up emotions on the sleepy Mexicans who were bumping into each other as they ran for the woods along the Bayou.

"Fire away!" Houston's voice was loud and clear.

Juan paused to reload. He saw the General's white horse sink to the ground; blood spattered Houston's clothes and saddle. In the confusion, the Mexican horses were running aimlessly in all directions. Juan managed to grab the reins of one and made his way to the General. The commander swung himself into the saddle and yelled, "Fire!"

Many of Santa Anna's men never reached their weapons, they ran screaming and empty handed into the trees with the Texans at their heels.

Blood trickled into General Houston's boot, a bullet had smashed into his leg. Juan heard him exclaim as he glanced at his watch, "Eighteen minutes — the battle is over!"

Later that evening, Juan Seguin stared at the dead and shook his head. For years Santa Anna's desire for greed and power had been a threat. How sad that one evil force was responsible for so much heartache and sadness. Juan thought of Gregario Esparza who died at the Alamo fighting against his own brother. Friend killing friend, countryman fighting countryman. All for one man's corrupt ambition! But where was Santa Anna? His body was not among the 600 dead or the 750 prisoners. Where was he?

General Houston lay propped against a tree with his wounded leg outstretched in front of him. "Boys," he commanded, "Bury the nine Texans and the others, but I want all prisoners brought to me. I want to see them!"

The prisoners moved forward for questioning. Suddenly, one of them cried, "*El Presidente!*" All turned to stare at a man dressed like a common soldier. "*El Presidente!*" several exclaimed.

Bedlam broke loose. Houston yelled, "Seguin, bring that man to me before someone tears him apart!"

Juan's hand shook, his soul trembled with emotion as he had to shield his enemy with his own body. For one brief moment Juan's eyes met Santa Anna's! Remembering the years of hate and fear, Juan closed his eyes and breathed deeply. It was over! The dictator had fallen.

Texas was free!

5

Keeping the Faith

News traveled fast. The war was over! After months of fighting and worry, there was new hope. Texas became a free Republic and Sam Houston was made the first President.

During the summer of 1836, settlers returned to claim their land and rebuild their homes destroyed by the war. Texan soldiers rejoined their families. Juan and his friend, Antonio Menchaca, rode to Nacogdoches for their wives and children. They found the town had not been spared from the difficulties of the war. Many people were ill from the crowded living conditions and lack of proper food.

Juan and his friend found their families half starved; most were sick with the fever that had killed many of the refugees. Juan grieved when he learned his son, José, his uncle and two other relatives had died from the disease. He was also unhappy to find that his father had sold everything of value for food and shelter. His family was not only thin and hungry, but very poor.

Juan traded one of his two rifles for a donkey to pull a cart his father had brought when they fled from Santa Anna. They borrowed an ox and wagon to start home. The trip was a nightmare. Juan caught the sickness and, like most of his family, was too ill to walk. Antonio was the only one strong enough to work and guide the wagon.

Finally, after a most difficult journey, the little band crossed the San Antonio River. Passing the ruins of the Alamo, they looked at the town. The wooden buildings had been destroyed or burned by Santa Anna's men after the Alamo had fallen. Only the thick walled adobe mud buildings remained. Slowly the little procession made its way down the street to stop in front of what remained of the Seguin *hacienda*. Much of the house had been destroyed, only the adobe shell remained.

The travelers climbed from the carts. Hot and thirsty, their first thoughts were of the cool water in the well. Juan put his arms around his father and said reassuringly, "Do not worry, *Papacito,* we will start again."

With the passing of time, life settled down to normal. The ill effects of war faded. Juan resumed his position as an important citizen of San Antonio. In recognition of his heroic service in the Revolution, General Sam Houston appointed Juan commander of the city.

After Santa Anna's defeat his army was forced to return to Mexico. Many people believed Santa Anna should have been executed, but Houston and others decided against that. Instead, he was made a prisoner of war and not allowed to return to Mexico until much later.

There were occasional rumors that the Mexicans were reorganizing their army to return. Mexico did not want to recognize Texas's Independence.

One morning early the next summer, a group of Texas soldiers rode into San Antonio. When notified of their arrival, Juan hurried to meet them and invite them to his home.

One of the older men stepped forward. "I am Colonel Switzer."

"Welcome, I am Juan Seguin. Won't you come in?"

The officer shook his head. "Sir, I have a message for you from our new commander, General Felix Huston." He reached into his pocket and took out a letter to give to Juan. He watched him break the wax seal and read the order.

Juan's face turned white with rage. "Never! Never!" He glared at the man. "Do you know what this says? I am to move the people to the east bank of the Brazos River and destroy this town!"

The Colonel nodded. "Yes, sir, I know. I was sent to help you."

"Help me?" Juan gritted his teeth and shook his fist. "I will never destroy this place. We withstood the Mexicans under Cos and were defeated under Santa Anna. Still San Antonio survived. We will not destroy the place because this General Huston orders it! You tell your General that." He turned on his heels and stormed into the cool shade of his house.

The colonel watched Juan disappear into the shadows and remounted his horse. "Let's ride to Houston and tell him, boys." They left a cloud of dust behind as they galloped down the street, past the lonely deserted fort to cross the San Antonio River.

Juan's face was pale with anger as he looked from his wife and mother to his father. "*Papacito,* send for my fastest horse! I am going to President Sam Houston to plead for our people. General Felix Huston wants to force us to move and burn our town!"

His father caught his breath. "What? After what our people have been through? Never! If there is trouble with Mexico again we will stay here and fight. We will not run, not again. You go tell Sam Houston that!"

A short time later Juan slowed his horse and looked at the lonely fortress of the Alamo. He remembered his comrades who had died for the cause of freedom. Silently he promised himself and his dead friends, *When I return I will see that your ashes have a proper burial. You will not have died in vain.*

Memories of other rides passed through Juan's thoughts as he galloped toward the town of Columbia where Houston had his Presidential offices.

The next day Juan met with the new President of Texas, his friend Sam Houston.

"Good to see you again, Seguin. What brings you here?"

Juan's handsome face clouded with emotion. "Sir, for the first time in my life I have refused to obey an order!"

The President frowned, "What kind of order? I didn't send one."

Juan reached into his pocket and handed him the message from Huston. He waited quietly while Houston read it. Juan's brown eyes met the other man's. "Sir, I couldn't obey that command, that is why I am here."

"You are a patriot tried and true, Seguin. You did the right thing in coming to me." Houston paused and rubbed the old bullet wound on his leg. From the expression on his face Juan knew the President was deep in thought. Finally, he cleared his throat and declared. "You go home, Seguin, and let me handle this fellow Huston. In confidence let me explain that this man brought five hundred men to Texas after the war and he has caused trouble ever since!" The President waved the paper and added, "This is just one more of the things he has done, but I'll take care of him."

Weeks after Juan's return home he learned the President had outsmarted Huston by offering his soldiers furloughs of leave along with a choice of land grants or free trips back to the U.S. The men accepted the offer. Huston found he was a general with no army. Juan felt relieved.

Shortly after his return, Juan had a message posted on the town's main plaza:

> ON FEBRUARY 23RD AFTER MASS WE WILL PAY
> FINAL RESPECTS TO OUR FRIENDS WHO DIED
> AT THE ALAMO.
>> JUAN SEGUIN,
>> COMMANDER LT. COL.

Following services in San Fernando Church that morning, a solemn processional of citizens gathered to walk behind those men carrying the newly made wooden coffin containing the ashes of the dead heroes. At the cemetery they stood in reverent silence beside the open grave and stared expressionless at the coffin. On a signal from Juan his men fired their rifles into the air. Muffled sobs mingled with whispered prayers.

"Citizens," Juan said. "Last year on March sixth, after thirteen days of battle, many brave men died at the Alamo. They were of different cultural backgrounds: Mexican, English, Scotch, French and American. But they had a common cause, freedom for Texas!" He paused and then continued. "They died to blaze our trail. Let us not forget the Alamo."

Juan watched men shovel black earth back into the hole to fill the grave. Antonio Oroche softly whistled the tune, *Will you Come to my Bower?* The sun broke through the clouds while birds trilled from a nearby tree.

51

One by one the people turned toward their homes. Juan looked from his mother and father to his wife and children. He thought of their tomorrows.

Silently, he turned away and mounted his horse. He rode past the lonely fortress, now silent and forsaken, and thought of Bowie, Travis, Esparza and the rest. He felt a surge of pride that he had been the friend and companion to such great heroes and had fought by their side to win freedom for Texas.

BIBLIOGRAPHY

JUVENILE

Callihan, Jeanne, *Our Mexican Ancestors, Volume One,* University of
   Texas Institute of Texan Cultures, San Antonio, 1981
Downey, Farfax, *Texas and the War with Mexico,* American Heritage
   Publishers, New York, 1961
Jaxon, *Recuerden El Alamo,* Last Gasp Publishers, Berkeley, Califor-
   nia, 1979
Kownslar, Alan O., *The Texans, their land and History,* McGraw–
   Hill, New York, 1978
Tinkle, Lon, *The Valiant Few,* MacMillan, New York, 1964

PERIODICALS

Markey, Carol, "Alamo burial site still a mystery," Sunday *San Antonio Express–News,* August 1, 1982
Ramsdell, Charles, "Casa Blanca," *San Antonio Express,* November
   21, 1948
Standush, Claude, "It's Curse of Veramendi," *San Antonio Express*

ADULTS

Brown, *History of Texas,* Volume I. Jenkins Publishing, Austin, 1970
Chabot, Frederick, *With the Makers of San Antonio,* Private Publish-
   ers, San Antonio, 1937
Nevin, David, *The Texans,* Time–Life Books, New York, 1975
Potter, Reuben M., *The Fall of The Alamo,* reprint by Otterden
   Press, HIllsdale, New Jersey, 1977
Seguin, John, *Personal Memoirs of John N. Seguin,* Ledger Book and
   Job, Offica, San Antonio, 1858
Steen, Ralph, *History of Texas,* Steck Company, Austin, Texas, 1939

Tinkle, Lon, *The Alamo*, New American Library, Inc. New York, 1958

Turner, Martha Anne, *TEXAS EPIC An American Story,* Nortex Press, Quanah, Wichita Falls, Texas 1974

Webb, Walter, *West Texas Historical Association Year Book,* Volume XXV, Abilene, Texas, 1949